D1399205

AUG   2012

Your Life as a CABIN ATTENDANT on the TITANIC

BY JESSICA GUNDERSON

ILLUSTRATED BY RACHEL DOUGHERTY

SKOKIE PUBLIC LIBRARY

Thanks to our advisers for their expertise, research, and advice:

Glenn Kranking, PhD, Assistant Professor of History & Scandinavian Studies
Gustavus Adolphus College, Saint Peter, Minnesota

Terry Flahery, PhD, Professor of English
Minnesota State University, Mankato

Editor: Jill Kalz
Designer: Ashlee Suker
Art Director: Nathan Gassman
Production Specialist: Danielle Ceminsky
The illustrations in this book were created with acrylics.

Picture Window Books
1710 Roe Crest Drive
North Mankato, MN 56003
www.capstonepub.com

Copyright © 2012 by Picture Window Books, a Capstone imprint.
All rights reserved. No part of this book may be reproduced without
written permission from the publisher. The publisher takes no
responsibility for the use of any of the materials or methods described
in this book, nor for the products thereof.

All books published by Picture Window Books
are manufactured with paper containing at least
10 percent post-consumer waste.

Library of Congress Cataloging-in-Publication Data
Gunderson, Jessica.
  Your life as a cabin attendant on the Titanic / by Jessica Gunderson ;
illustrated by Rachel Dougherty.
      p. cm. — (The way it was)
  Includes index.
  ISBN 978-1-4048-7158-8 (library binding)
  ISBN 978-1-4048-7248-6 (paperback)
  1. Titanic (Steamship)—Juvenile literature. 2. Shipwrecks—North
Atlantic Ocean—Juvenile literature. I. Dougherty, Rachel, 1988– ill.
II. Title.
  G530.T6.G86 2012
  910.9163'4—dc23   2011029573

Printed in the United States of America in North Mankato, Minnesota.
102011   006405CGS12

YOUR ROLE

Congratulations! You'll be playing the role of Mary Thomas in our play "Life on *Titanic*." It's April 10, 1912, in Southampton, England. You're a 20-year-old woman about to set sail aboard RMS *Titanic* on its very first voyage. You'll be working as a cabin attendant, or steward, waiting on passengers. You'll put their needs before your own, even in the face of danger. What? *Danger,* you say?

No time to explain. **Ready?**

All aboard!

Sailing Day

You're gathered on *Titanic*'s deck with more than 300 other stewards and service crew. The head steward is shouting instructions, but you're barely listening. You're excited to see the inside of the ship. All the newspapers have been talking about the unsinkable steamship *Titanic* and its first voyage across the Atlantic Ocean. You can't wait to set sail!

The White Star Line's *Titanic* was about 883 feet (269 meters) long and 93 feet (28 m) wide. It stood about 60 feet (18 m) tall from the water line. It carried 2,223 passengers and crew.

You're one of just **18 female stewards** on the ship. *Surprised?* Sailors back then didn't want women on board a ship, especially as workers. They thought it was **bad luck**.

CRAMPED QUARTERS

The head steward leads you to a tiny cabin. You'll share it with three other women. The bunks are narrow, with a single washbowl between them. You groan. But one of the women, Annie, says, **"Wow! This is huge compared to other ships I've been on. We have our own lockers!"**

You all pull on your uniforms. It's tough not to bump into each other. You apologize repeatedly, then head out to the hallway.

Stewards brought their own uniforms. They wore a special numbered pin that showed they were part of the crew.

About 900 workers helped keep *Titanic* running smoothly. They included officers, stewards, chefs, mailroom staff, engine room men, and more.

GRAND TOUR

Before you begin work, the head steward gives you a quick tour. He leads you into the first-class dining room. A chandelier glitters above a large curved staircase. **"It's like a palace on water!"** Annie exclaims.

The head steward points at the elevators next to you. **"Those elevators lead to the first-class cabins,"** he says. You reach to press the button, but he yells, **"Stop!"** You pull your hand back. **"Only first-class passengers can use them,"** he explains.

Want to sit down, Mary? Don't try to slide out a chair. All furniture is **bolted** to the floor to keep it from sliding as the ship moves.

First-Class Style

You walk downstairs to the first-class cabins. They're lovely. Rich passengers are treated to carved wooden beds, fancy glass lamps, and electric heaters. The beds look so soft, and you and Annie are so tired. Annie wants to lie down, just to see what it would be like. **"Don't!"** you hiss. **"Here come the passengers!"**

Some people nod at you as they board. Most look right past you. Even their servants seem snobby.

The most expensive first-class fare was $4,375. That's almost $100,000 today.

One Big Ship

You don't know how you're going to find your way around this giant ship. It's a maze!

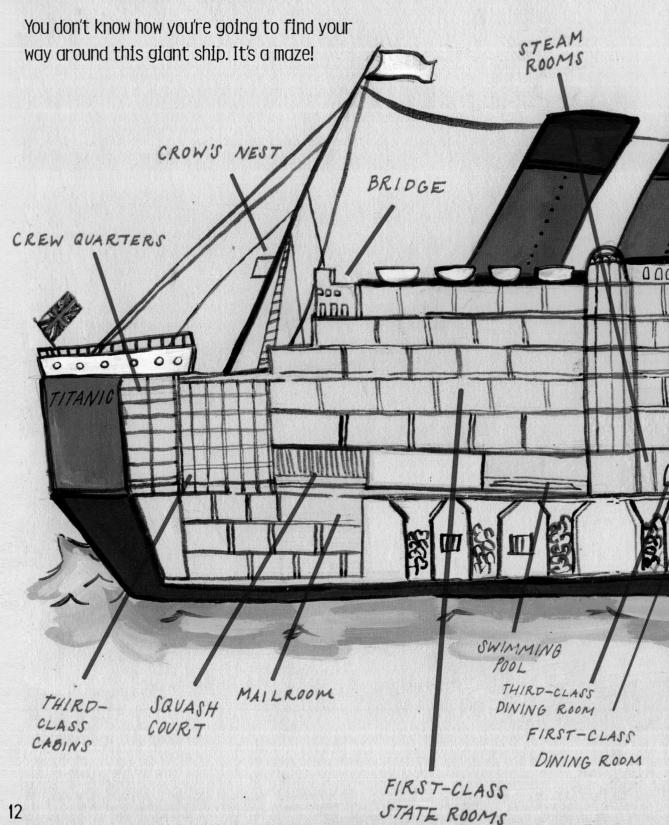

STEAM ROOMS

CROW'S NEST

BRIDGE

CREW QUARTERS

TITANIC

THIRD-CLASS CABINS

SQUASH COURT

MAILROOM

SWIMMING POOL

THIRD-CLASS DINING ROOM

FIRST-CLASS DINING ROOM

FIRST-CLASS STATE ROOMS

The first-class area is just the start. There are also second- and third-class areas, a gym, a swimming pool, and special steam rooms. There's even a court for playing a ball-and-racket game called squash.

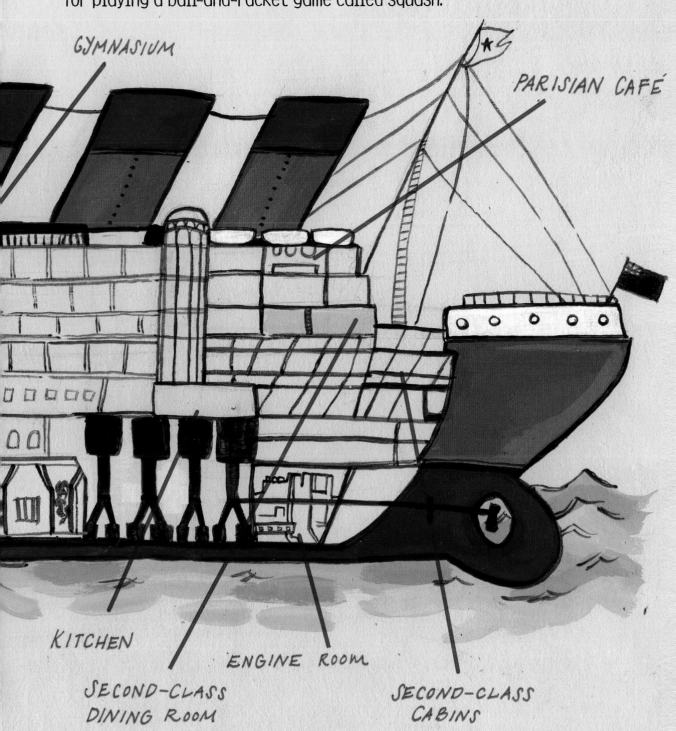

GYMNASIUM

PARISIAN CAFÉ

KITCHEN

ENGINE ROOM

SECOND-CLASS
DINING ROOM

SECOND-CLASS
CABINS

A Day's Work

The ship hasn't even reached open ocean yet, and your passengers are already demanding things: fresh towels, cold drinks, hot drinks, snacks ... They ask questions and complain a lot.

"Where's the café?"

"My room is hot!"

"My coffee is cold!"

"Where's the smoking room?"

First-class passengers were served fancy 10-course meals. They dined on steak, shrimp, lamb, creamy soups, and ice cream. Third-class passengers ate much simpler food, including oatmeal, eggs, and roast beef with gravy.

SWEET SECOND-CLASS

A passenger asks you to carry a letter to the mailroom. On your way to the ship's hold, you pass the second-class cabins. They're comfortable and roomy but not as fine as first-class.

You see a steward named Robert trying to unlock a door to the third-class area. Unable to balance an armload of towels, he yells, **"Grab these!"** You obey and follow him down into third-class.

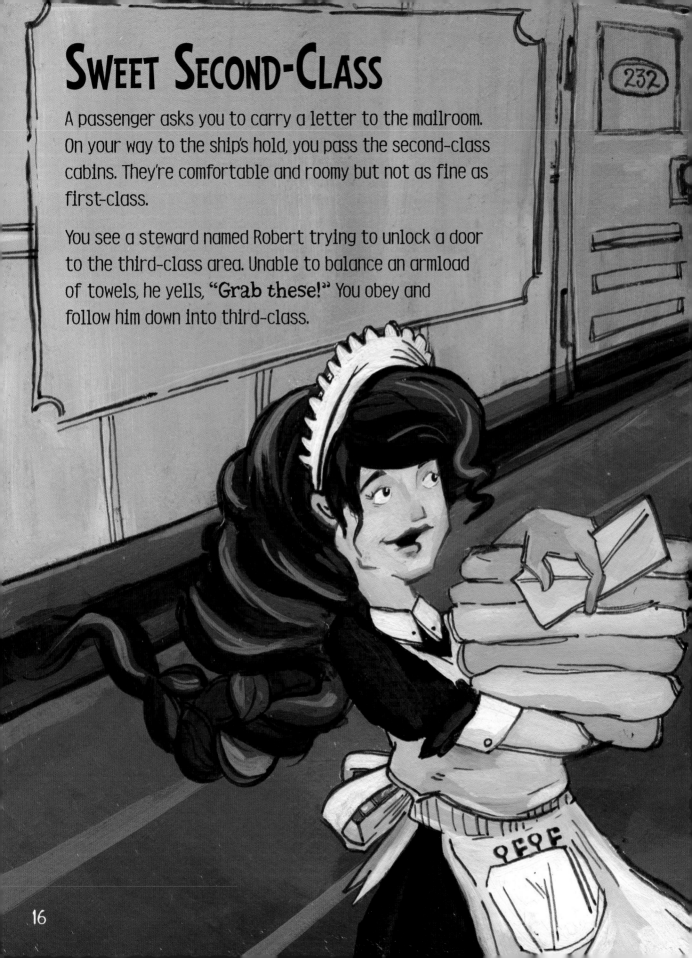

MAIL

Titanic's official name was RMS *Titanic*. The letters RMS stand for "Royal Mail Ship." *Titanic* carried mail from England to the United States.

Second-class travel on *Titanic* was better than first-class on many other ships. The oak-paneled dining room served four-course meals. Second-class passengers also had their own library, lounges, and one elevator.

HAPPY TRAVELERS

Third-class, or steerage, is noisy and crowded. At the bow, a room holds many beds for men traveling alone. Single women sleep in cabins at the back. Families are crammed into small cabins along the hall. Polish, Swedish, and other languages you don't speak fill the air. **"Everyone here seems happier than the first-class passengers,"** you say. Robert smiles. **"They aren't used to luxury,"** he says. **"Many are just glad for a bed to sleep in."**

More than half of *Titanic's* passengers traveled third-class. Many were immigrating to the United States. According to immigration laws, locked doors had to separate immigrants from other passengers.

The lowest third-class fare was $36.25, about $800 today. That may sound cheap compared to first-class. But it was more money than many third-class passengers made in a year.

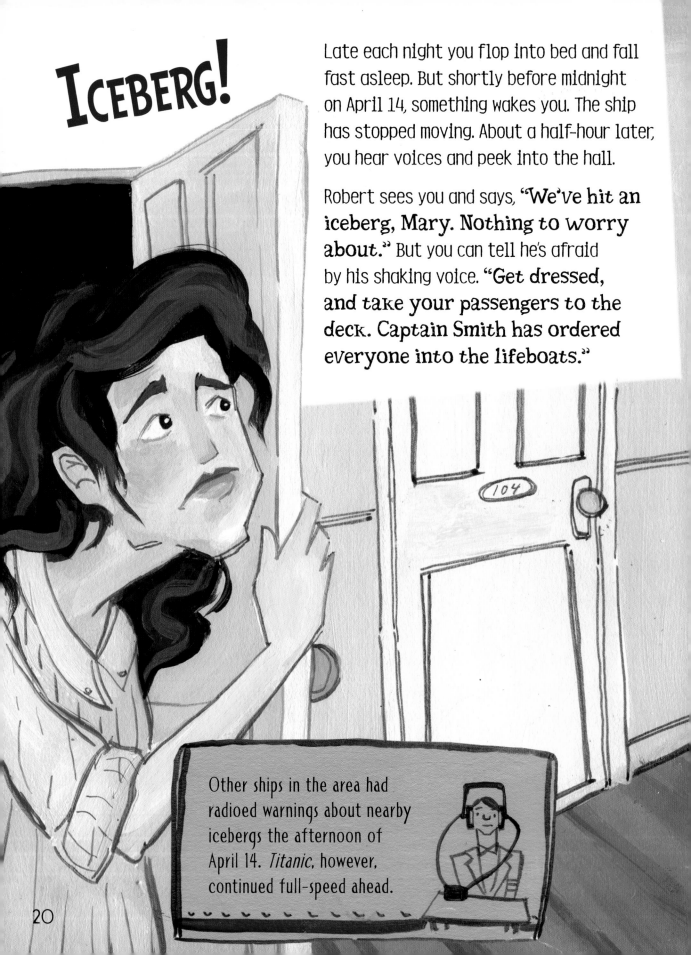

ICEBERG!

Late each night you flop into bed and fall fast asleep. But shortly before midnight on April 14, something wakes you. The ship has stopped moving. About a half-hour later, you hear voices and peek into the hall.

Robert sees you and says, **"We've hit an iceberg, Mary. Nothing to worry about."** But you can tell he's afraid by his shaking voice. **"Get dressed, and take your passengers to the deck. Captain Smith has ordered everyone into the lifeboats."**

Other ships in the area had radioed warnings about nearby icebergs the afternoon of April 14. *Titanic*, however, continued full-speed ahead.

Frederick Fleet, a lookout on *Titanic's* crow's nest, spotted an iceberg and rang the warning bell. The officer at the wheel tried to turn, but the iceberg sliced the right side of the ship.

Don't forget to put on your lifejacket, Mary. If you put yours on, other passengers will be more willing to do so too.

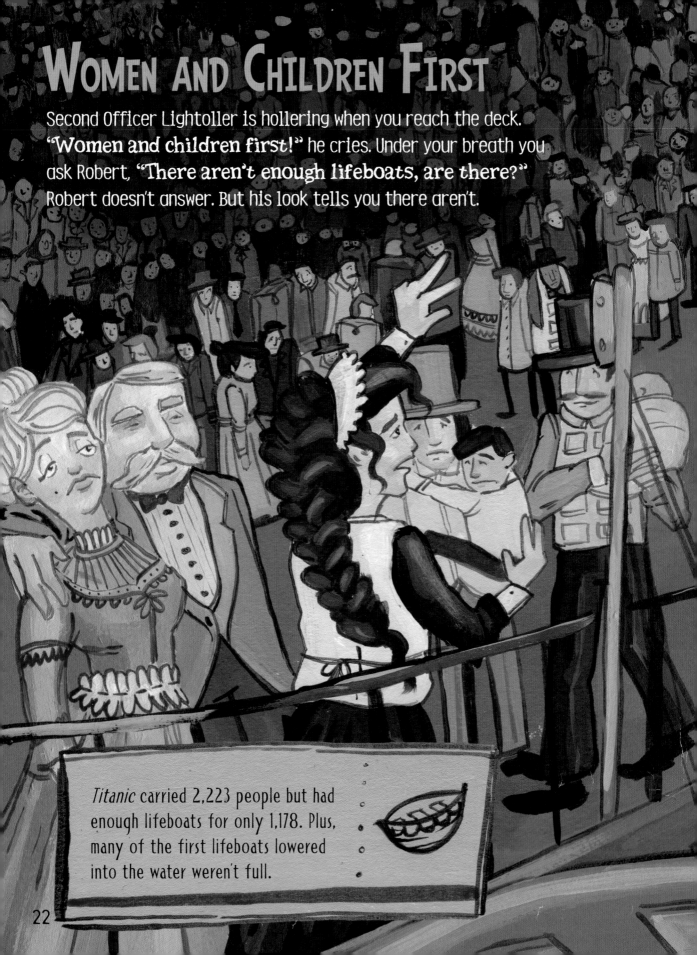

WOMEN AND CHILDREN FIRST

Second Officer Lightoller is hollering when you reach the deck. **"Women and children first!"** he cries. Under your breath you ask Robert, **"There aren't enough lifeboats, are there?"** Robert doesn't answer. But his look tells you there aren't.

Titanic carried 2,223 people but had enough lifeboats for only 1,178. Plus, many of the first lifeboats lowered into the water weren't full.

You start helping women into a lifeboat. Signal rockets blaze. Some women cry, not wanting to leave their husbands. **"Someone will come for us,"** you assure them, smiling. **"No worries now.** *Titanic's* **unsinkable, remember?"** But you can feel the ship slanting beneath your feet. And where are all the third-class passengers?

Many third-class passengers couldn't get to the lifeboats. Doors to the upper decks were locked. One steward, William Cox, led some third-class passengers to safety. He later died.

Last Chance

It's been about an hour and a half since you woke. There aren't many lifeboats left, and hundreds of people are still on board. Robert hurries toward you. **"Get in,"** he says, shoving you and Annie toward Lifeboat 14. **"What about you?"** you ask, but he has already hustled away. You won't see him again.

You and Annie cling to each other as the lifeboat is lowered into the dark, frothy water below. Your teeth chatter in the cold.

Some passengers later became famous for their bravery. The "Unsinkable" Molly Brown was a first-class passenger who helped people into lifeboats. The Countess of Rothes took charge of steering a lifeboat all night.

THE UNSINKABLE SINKS

You and the other passengers take turns rowing away from *Titanic*.

The band played until *Titanic* sank. The musicians thought music would keep the passengers' spirits up. All eight band members died.

The sinking ship is pulling nearby people and objects underwater with it. Annie gasps. You see the stern of *Titanic* rising into the air. The lights glow. "**I can still hear music!**" you say. Then the lights go out. All is dark. *Titanic* cracks in two and in minutes sinks for good.

"**We have to look for survivors,**" someone says. You agree. And you do manage to pull a few people aboard.

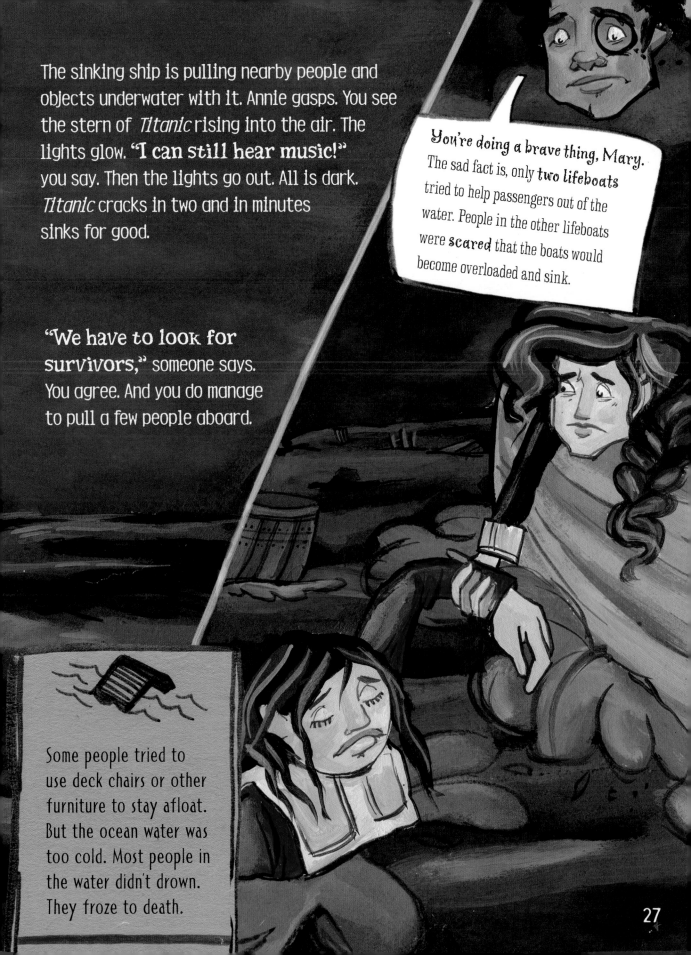

You're doing a brave thing, Mary. The sad fact is, only **two lifeboats** tried to help passengers out of the water. People in the other lifeboats were **scared** that the boats would become overloaded and sink.

Some people tried to use deck chairs or other furniture to stay afloat. But the ocean water was too cold. Most people in the water didn't drown. They froze to death.

RESCUE!

Around four o'clock, you hear the blare of a horn. A ship appears.
It's *Carpathia*. You wave frantically, and the sailors spot you.
Once on board, you and Annie wrap yourselves in blankets.
You're safe, but you know more than 1,000 others aren't.

Carpathia was 58 miles (93 km) away when the crew heard *Titanic's* calls. The ship raced to help but didn't arrive until three and a half hours later. Another ship, *Californian*, was close by but didn't hear the call.

Hours later, you think about all the lost lives as *Carpathia* steams toward New York. You'll never forget *Titanic*, the dream ship, the unsinkable ship, disappearing into its dark, watery grave.

Only 705 people survived the sinking of *Titanic* on April 15, 1912. More than 1,500 died. Sixty percent of the total survivors came from first-class. Only 24 percent of the crew survived.

FINALE

What a bold, brave performance, Mary! You survived the sinking of *Titanic*.

But I'm afraid you won't get paid for your work. Most of the crew on *Titanic* never received a final paycheck. However, the White Star Line will hire you on another ship, if you want. **No way! you say**? Well, I don't blame you.

GLOSSARY

bow—the front end of a ship

crow's nest—a platform near the top of a ship's mast

hold— the storage area below the deck

immigrate—to leave one country and settle in another

steamship—a ship powered by a steam engine

stern—the back end of a ship

steward—a person who attends to passengers' needs

INDEX

MORE BOOKS TO READ

Benoit, Peter. *The Titanic Disaster.* A True Book. New York: Children's Press, 2011.

Brown, Don. *All Stations! Distress!: April 15, 1912, the Day the Titanic Sank.* New York: Flash Point/Roaring Brook Press, 2008.

Temple, Bob. *The Titanic: An Interactive History Adventure.* You Choose Books. Mankato, Minn.: Capstone Press, 2008.

INTERNET SITES

FactHound offers a safe, fun way to find Internet sites related to this book. All of the sites on FactHound have been researched by our staff.

Here's all you do:

Visit *www.facthound.com*

Type in this code: 9781404871588

 Check out projects, games and lots more at
www.capstonekids.com

LOOK FOR ALL THE BOOKS IN THE SERIES: